Marvel

Recipes

Amazing Single Serving Meals!

BY

Daniel Humphreys

License Notes

No part of this Book can be reproduced in any form or by any means including print, electronic, scanning or photocopying unless prior permission is granted by the author.

All ideas, suggestions and guidelines mentioned here are written for informative purposes. While the author has taken every possible step to ensure accuracy, all readers are advised to follow information at their own risk. The author cannot be held responsible for personal and/or commercial damages in case of misinterpreting and misunderstanding any part of this Book

Table of Contents

Introduction

If you're trying to think of ways to spend less time in the kitchen but make delicious snacks, desserts and even single serving meals then here is your chance. I have included very simple yet delicious recipes in this book that you can enjoy in no time.

You may even find some inspiration and put some twist on these recipes yourself. Cook up some healthy brown rice with edamame or a sugary molten chocolate cake, you can do it all! What's even better is that because these recipes are single serving, you can customize them to meet the needs of multiple people; you can make a mug brownie for yourself, a funfetti cake for a friend and a red velvet cake for your family member, not to mention prep and clean-up is a breeze!

Omelette

Eggs, cheese and peppers, what else could make a better breakfast? This omelette in a mug is delicious and you can fill it up with whatever meat or veggies you like!

Cooking time: 2 minutes

Ingredients:

- 2 eggs, lightly whisked
- 1 tablespoon of milk
- 1 teaspoon of cooking oil or butter
- 1 tablespoon of red peppers
- 1 tablespoon of feta cheese
- 1 teaspoon of finely chopped green onions
- Salt and pepper to taste

Instructions:

1. Coat inside of mug with cooking oil or butter.

2. Add ingredients to mug and gently stir.

3. Microwave for 1 minute 30 seconds, or until done. Let sit for 1 minute.

Pancake in a Mug

No need to heat up a pan and stand up scooping batter, you can have a warm, fluffy pancake in a mug in no time. Top with some maple syrup and fresh fruit and no one will ever know you barely did anything to make this!

Cooking time: 2 minutes

Ingredients:

- ½ cup of pancake mix
- ½ cup of milk
- 1 cup of blueberries

Instructions:

1. Combine pancake mix and milk until smooth.

2. Fold in blueberries.

3. Microwave for 1 minute 30 seconds – 2 minutes, until done.

Egg Breakfast Sandwich

Breakfast sandwiches are a flavourful, handy breakfast choice and you can make the egg filling for your sandwich right in the microwave. Top with some slices of avocado and a sprinkle of cheese and this is a nutrient packed quick meal.

Cooking time: 2 minutes

Ingredients:

- 1 large egg
- 1 tablespoon of milk
- 1 – 2 tablespoons of ham, finely chopped
- 1 tablespoon of green bell pepper
- 1 teaspoon of butter, melted
- Salt and pepper to taste

Instructions:

1. Combine egg, milk, butter and salt and pepper in a bowl and beat well.

2. Add ham and green pepper and pour into mug. Cover mug with a paper towel and microwave for 1 minute 30 seconds, until the mixture is solid throughout.

3. Allow to cool for 30 seconds.

4. Place egg between an English muffin and top with desired toppings.

Vegan Scramble

Breakfast isn't only about the eggs. This delicious tofu scramble is filling, packed with veggies and a great start to your day.

Cooking time: 2 minutes

Ingredients:

- ½ block of tofu, crumbled
- 1 tablespoon of soy sauce
- 1 teaspoon of curry powder
- ¼ teaspoon of garlic, finely chopped
- ½ cup of nutritional yeast
- ½ tablespoon of lemon juice
- 1 cup of spinach
- 1 cup of mushrooms, roughly chopped
- Salt and pepper to taste

Instructions:

1. Combine all ingredients in mug.

2. Microwave for 1 – 2 minutes, until done.

French Toast

Another breakfast classic that you can make while heading out the door in the mornings. No need to heat up a pan, just throw all your ingredients in a mug and you're set in 2 minutes! You can top with powdered sugar, maple syrup or fresh fruit.

Cooking time: 1 – 2 minutes

Ingredients:

- 2 slices of bread, cubes
- ½ teaspoon of cinnamon
- ½ teaspoon of sugar
- 4 tablespoons of milk
- 1 tablespoon of butter, melted
- 1 egg, beaten
- ¼ teaspoon of vanilla

Instructions:

1. Combine butter, milk, cinnamon, sugar, vanilla and egg in a bowl.

2. Add cubes of bread to mug and pour cinnamon mixture over bread, let sit for 10 – 20 seconds for the bread to soak up the mixture.

3. Microwave for 1 – 2 minutes until set.

Oatmeal

Oatmeal is a warm, hardy breakfast option and so so simple to make. This recipe is a cinnamon apple version but this can be done with your favourite flavours such as blueberries or strawberries and cream.

Cooking time: 5 minutes

Ingredients:

- 1 cup of rolled oats
- 1 small apple, peeled, cored and chopped
- 1 teaspoon of cinnamon
- ½ teaspoon of ground nutmeg
- 1 – 1 ¼ cups of water
- 1 tablespoon of sweetened condensed milk
- 1 tablespoon of brown sugar or maple syrup
- Salt to taste

Instructions:

1. Mix together condensed milk and water. Add cinnamon, nutmeg, brown sugar / maple syrup and salt to milk and mix well.

2. Pour mixture onto oats and apples in a bowl. Stir well.

3. Add to mug and microwave for 5 – 8 minutes until done, this is when apples are soft and the oats have absorbed the liquid.

Spinach Quiche

Here's your chance to make a fluffy quiche packed with spinach and cheese that's great for breakfast. This quiche comes together so quickly and is sure to be a favourite.

Cooking time: 3 minutes

Ingredients:

- 1 egg
- ½ cup of frozen spinach, drained and roughly chopped
- ¼ cup milk
- 1 tablespoon of red bell pepper, finely chopped
- Salt and pepper to taste

Instructions:

1. Whisk egg, milk and salt and pepper together in a mug.

2. Mix in red bell pepper and spinach until well combined.

3. Cover with a paper towel folded in half and microwave for 3 minutes, or until cooked through.

Pumpkin Pie Breakfast

This pumpkin pie is perfect for breakfast; it's warm, filling and a nice mini version of a tasty dessert. It's packed with quinoa and has a great cinnamon-holiday flavour that will just help to give you a great start to your day. You can top with nut butter and chopped nuts.

Cooking time: 3 minutes

Ingredients:

- ¼ cup of cooked quinoa
- ¼ cup of pumpkin puree
- 1 large egg
- ¼ teaspoon of pumpkin pie spice
- 2 teaspoons of sugar
- ¼ teaspoon of vanilla
- ¼ teaspoon of salt

Instructions:

1. Combine ingredients in a bowl. Mix until well combined.

2. Pour batter into a mug.

3. Microwave for 3 minutes or until cake is done and center is cooked through.

Granola in a Mug

Granola is a healthy, delicious snack that can be enjoyed with just about anything, with some fresh / dried fruit or some yogurt it doesn't matter. And this granola is sweet and delicious.

Cooking time: 2 minutes

Ingredients:

- 5 tablespoons of rolled oats
- 1 tablespoon of coconut flakes
- 1 tablespoon of pecans
- 1 tablespoon of sliced almonds
- 1 ½ tablespoons of honey
- 2 teaspoons of water
- 2 teaspoons of vegetable oil
- A pinch of salt

Instructions:

1. Combine ingredients in a mug and microwave for 1 minute 30 seconds. Stir.

2. Microwave for another minute until oats are golden brown.

3. Allow to cool.

Coconut Cinnamon Roll

Enjoy a warm, gooey cinnamon roll with a twist – coconut! You would've never believed coconut and cinnamon go so well together, they're the perfect companion.

Cooking time: 2 minutes

Ingredients:

- ¼ cup of coconut flour
- 1 teaspoon of cinnamon
- ¼ teaspoon of nutmeg
- ¾ teaspoon of vanilla
- ¾ teaspoon of baking powder
- 1 egg
- 3 – 4 tablespoons of coconut milk
- 2 tablespoons of brown sugar
- 1 ½ tablespoons of coconut oil
- 3 tablespoons of frosting, melted
- Coconut flakes

Instructions:

1. Combine dry ingredients (except baking powder) in a bowl then add wet ingredients. Mix until smooth. Add baking powder and mix.

2. Pour batter into a mug.

3. Microwave for 2 minutes or until cake is done and cooked through.

4. Drizzle icing on top in a spiral design and top with coconut flakes.

Burrito Mug

Beans, salsa, rice, corn chips... all you need in a burrito but much more convenient since it's in a mug! You can customize this recipe with whatever toppings and filling you like.

Prep time: 3 minutes

Ingredients:

- ½ cup of rice, cooked
- ¼ cup of black bean, drained
- 2 tablespoons of salsa
- A few corn chips
- 2 tablespoons of avocado, diced
- Salt to taste

Instructions:

1. Add rice, black beans and salsa to mug, stir.

2. Microwave for 1 minute to warm it up. Season with salt.

3. Top with corn chips and diced avocado.

Mug Pizza

Yes, you read right… pizza! A real pizza that's easy to make and can serve a bunch of people for any occasion. You can spice it up with whatever toppings you like.

Cooking time: 2 minutes

Ingredients:

- ¼ cup of all-purpose flour
- ¼ teaspoon of baking powder
- 3 ½ tablespoons of milk
- 1 tablespoon olive oil
- 2 tablespoons marinara sauce
- 2 tablespoons mozzarella, shredded
- 7 – 10 mini pepperonis
- ¾ teaspoon of dried Italian herbs
- A pinch of baking soda
- A generous pinch of salt

Instructions:

1. Combine flour, baking powder, baking soda and salt in mug. Mix in milk and olive oil.

2. Add marinara sauce, spread it evenly over batter.

3. Sprinkle with cheese, add pepperoni and Italian herbs.

4. Microwave for 1 minute, or until the pizza rises and the cheese is bubbling.

Mac and Cheese

You can enjoy delicious, cheesy mac and cheese in just a few minutes, without the stove. This single serving is perfect for a very hungry kid, or an adult when they have a hankering for a childhood favourite. This is even more delicious because it's not the box version!

Cooking time: 5 minutes

Ingredients:

- 1 cup of elbow macaroni
- 1 ½ cups of water
- ¼ cup of milk
- 1 tablespoon of butter
- 3 tablespoons of cheddar cheese
- 2 tablespoons of mozzarella cheese
- Salt and pepper to taste

Instructions:

1. Combine water and macaroni in a large microwavable bowl. Cook on high for 3 minutes, or until pasta is done. Drain excess water.

2. Add macaroni to a large mug, stir in milk, butter, cheese, salt and pepper.

3. Microwave for an additional minute, until cheese has melted.

Brown Rice with Edamame

A delicious side option, you can pair it with more veggies or some meat. You can even add some pineapples for a sweet touch.

Cooking time: 5 minutes

Ingredients:

- ½ cup brown rice
- 2/3 cups of water
- ½ cup frozen edamame
- 1 tablespoon soy sauce
- 1 small onion, finely chopped
- A pinch of salt

Instructions:

1. Combine rice, water and salt in mug. Top with onions and edamame.

2. Microwave covered with paper towel for 3 – 4 minutes, drain excess water. Let stand for 1 minute.

3. Stir in soy sauce. Microwave for 45 seconds – 1 minute. Let stand for

Lasagna

Enjoy all the beautiful flavours of a classic lasagna in mini version. All you need is 2 minutes and you can enjoy a quick lasagna meal.

Cooking time: 4 minutes

Ingredients:

- 2 lasagna pasta sheets, cooked
- 4 tablespoons of pizza sauce
- 4 tablespoons of ricotta cheese
- 1 tablespoon of mozzarella, grated
- 3 tablespoons of spinach, roughly chopped
- 4 tablespoons of cooked sausage, chopped

Instructions:

1. To begin, add a layer of pizza sauce to bottom of mug. Add a layer of pasta, spinach, sausage and ricotta. To continue the layers, add pasta sheet, sauce, spinach, sausage and ricotta, repeat until ingredients are all used up.

2. Top with mozzarella and cook for 2 minutes 30 seconds – 4 minutes, until cheese has melted, and all the ingredients come together nicely.

3. Make sure to watch your mug so that the ingredients don't overflow or burn. Cool slightly before eating.

White Rice

Steamed white rice is the perfect companion to any main dish. This white rice made in the microwave is soft, fluffy and amazing. You can make it with beef or chicken broth to add a bit more flavour, but plain water is fine.

Cooking time: 8 – 10 minutes

Ingredients:

- ½ cup of white rice, washed
- 1 cup of water
- 2 teaspoons of butter / margarine
- Salt to taste

Instructions:

1. Combine all of the ingredients in a bowl with a tight cover.

2. Microwave covered for 5 minutes, until butter has melted and stir.

3. Microwave covered for an additional 2 – 3 minutes, until rice is done. Let sit covered for 1 – 2 minutes.

'Fried' Rice

You can make flavourful fried rice, (that's not actually fried but tastes just as good) right in a mug in your microwave. You can even fill it up with whatever veggies you like.

Cooking time: 3 minutes

Ingredients:

- ½ cup rice, cooked
- 1 tablespoon frozen mixed vegetables (peas, carrots, corn), cooked and drained
- 1 tablespoon red bell pepper, chopped
- 1 stalk of green onion, finely chopped
- 1 egg
- 1 tablespoon of soy sauce
- ½ teaspoon sesame oil
- ½ teaspoon onion powder
- Salt to taste

Instructions:

1. Add rice, vegetables, red bell pepper and green onion to mug in layers. Cover with a paper towel and cook for 30 seconds - 1 minute, until peppers arc soft.

2. Beat egg with sesame oil, onion powder, salt and soy sauce. Pour into mug and mix with rice and vegetables.

3. Cover mug again and microwave for 1 minute, stir rice mixture and microwave again for another 1 – 2 minutes until egg is cooked. Let rice stand for one minute.

Steamed Vegetables

You can steam some of your favourite veggies in the microwave and have them ready for your dinner plate in no time.

Cooking time: 5 – 7 minutes

Ingredients:

- ¼ cup of broccoli, cut into small florets
- 1 small carrot, cut into chunks
- ½ teaspoon of olive oil
- 1 – 2 tablespoons of water
- Salt to taste

Instructions:

1. Combine ingredients in a bowl.

2. Transfer mixture to a mug, cover with a paper towel folded in half.

3. Microwave for 4 – 5 minutes, until vegetables reach desired doneness.

Blueberry Mug Cake

This mug cake is great during breakfast as a breakfast muffin. This can be made with fresh or frozen blueberries, whatever your choice it is still delicious!

Cooking time: 2 minutes

Ingredients:

- ¼ cup all-purpose flour
- 1 medium egg
- 2 tablespoons of sugar
- 4 tablespoons of milk
- 1 tablespoons of butter, melted
- 1 teaspoon of vanilla
- ¼ teaspoon of baking powder
- ¼ cup of blueberries
- 1 tablespoon of lemon zest
- 1 teaspoon of lemon juice
- A pinch of salt

Instructions:

1. Combine dry ingredients in a bowl then add wet ingredients. Mix until smooth.

2. Pour batter into a mug.

3. Microwave for 1 minute 30 seconds or until cake is done and cooked through.

Peach Cobbler

The perfect combination of sweet peaches and a fluffy, moist cake. A great fruit dessert that when topped with some vanilla ice cream is to die for!

Cooking time: 3 minutes

Ingredients:

- ½ cup of peaches in syrup, drain most of the syrup
- ¼ cup white cake mix
- 1/8 teaspoon of cinnamon
- 3 tablespoons of milk
- 1 tablespoon of butter, melted

Instructions:

1. Combine cake mix and cinnamon, then add milk and butter. Mix until smooth.

2. Pour batter into a mug and add peaches on top, do not mix.

3. Microwave for 3 – 4 minutes until cake is done.

Apple Pie

Good ol' apple pie... but in a mug! Still an amazing treat but with less of the work and clean up. It's everything a good apple pie is; soft apples and a great cinnamon flavour.

Cooking time: 2 minutes

Ingredients:

- ½ cup of all-purpose flour
- ¼ cup apple pie filling
- 4 tablespoons of sugar
- ½ teaspoon of baking powder
- ¼ cup of milk
- 4 tablespoons of butter, melted
- ½ teaspoon of cinnamon
- 1 teaspoon of vanilla
- A pinch of salt
- A sprinkle of cinnamon sugar

Instructions:

1. Combine dry ingredients in a bowl then add wet ingredients and peanuts. Mix until smooth.

2. Spoon half of the batter into a mug, add half of the apple pie filling. Repeat this step with remaining batter and filling.

3. Sprinkle with cinnamon sugar.

4. Microwave for 1 minute 30 seconds or until cake is done and cooked through

Funfetti Mug Cake

This mug cake is not only colourful but it is moist, fluffy and sweet with a lovely vanilla flavour. Top with a scoop of ice cream or whipped cream to make it even better.

Cooking time: 2 minutes

Ingredients:

- 1 medium egg
- 2 tablespoons of sugar
- ¼ cup of all-purpose flour
- 1 tablespoons of butter, melted
- ¼ teaspoon of baking powder
- 4 tablespoons of milk
- ½ teaspoon cinnamon
- 1 teaspoon of vanilla
- ¼ teaspoon of almond extract
- 2 tablespoons of rainbow sprinkles
- A pinch of salt

Instructions:

1. Combine dry ingredients in a bowl then add wet ingredients. Mix until smooth.

2. Pour batter into a mug.

3. Microwave for 1 minute 30 seconds or until cake is done and cooked through.

Red Velvet Mug Cake

Great for the red velvet cake lovers out there who need a quick fixing! The mug cake is not only cute but it is also moist, chocolately and delicious.

Cooking time: 2 minutes

Ingredients:

- 5 tablespoons of all-purpose flour
- 2 tablespoons of cocoa powder
- 4 tablespoons of sugar
- ¼ teaspoon of baking powder
- 3 ½ tablespoons of oil
- 3 ½ tablespoons of buttermilk
- 1 egg
- ½ teaspoon red food colouring
- 2 – 3 tablespoons of cream cheese frosting

Instructions:

1. Combine dry ingredients in a bowl then add wet ingredients. Mix until smooth.

2. Pour batter into a large mug.

3. Microwave for 2 minutes or until cake is done and cooked through.

4. Top with cream cheese frosting.

Banana Muffin

A delicious mug muffin with a lovely banana flavour, the crunch of peanuts and a sweet cinnamon flavour. You can top with caramel and/ or ice cream if you really have a sweet tooth.

Cooking time: 2 minutes

Ingredients:

- ¼ cup of all-purpose flour
- 3 tablespoons of sugar
- 4 tablespoons of milk
- 1 tablespoon of butter, melted
- 1 medium egg
- ½ teaspoon of cinnamon
- 1 teaspoon of peanut butter (optional)
- ¼ teaspoon of nutmeg
- ¼ teaspoon of baking powder
- 1 ripe banana, crushed with a fork
- 1 teaspoon of vanilla
- 2 tablespoons of peanuts, chopped
- A pinch of salt

Instructions:

1. Combine dry ingredients in a bowl then add wet ingredients and peanuts. Mix until smooth.

2. Pour batter into a mug.

3. Microwave for 1 minute 30 seconds or until cake is done and cooked through

Cookies and Cream

Great in ice cream form and just as great as a warm cake. The crushed Oreos add a nice crunch and chocolate flavour.

Cooking time: 2 minutes

Ingredients:

- 5 tablespoons all-purpose flour
- 3 Oreo cookies, crushed
- ¼ cup white chocolate chips, melted
- 3 ½ tablespoons milk
- ½ teaspoon baking powder
- 1 teaspoon of sugar
- 1 teaspoon oil

Instructions:

1. Combine milk and white chocolate chips in mug. Add remaining ingredients, mix until smooth.

2. Microwave for 1 minute, or until done.

3. Let cool.

Chocolate Mug Cake

This chocolate mug cake is moist and oh so delicious. You can also add some mini chocolate chips in the batter for a burst of melted chocolate in each bite. You can top with vanilla ice cream or marshmallow fluff.

Cooking time: 2 minutes

Ingredients:

- ¼ cup of all-purpose flour
- 1 medium egg
- 3 tablespoons of sugar
- 4 tablespoons of milk
- 1 tablespoon of butter, melted
- 1 teaspoon of peanut butter (optional)
- ¼ teaspoon baking powder
- 1 teaspoon of vanilla
- 2 tablespoons of cocoa powder
- ¼ cup of mini chocolate chips
- A pinch of salt

Instructions:

1. Combine dry ingredients in a bowl then add wet ingredients. Mix until smooth.

2. Pour batter into a mug.

3. Microwave for 1 minute 30 seconds or until cake is done and cooked through.

Molten Chocolate Mug Cake

Forget ordering food and getting that generic lava cake, you can make your own delicious molten chocolate cake in a flash that's way more authentic and much tastier.

Cooking time: 2 minutes

Ingredients:

- ¼ cup of all-purpose flour
- 1 medium egg
- 4 tablespoons of sugar
- ½ teaspoon of baking powder
- 4 tablespoons of milk
- 2 tablespoons of butter, melted
- 1 teaspoon of vanilla
- 2 tablespoons of cocoa powder
- ¼ cup of mini chocolate chips
- 1 tablespoon water
- A pinch of salt

Instructions:

1. Combine dry ingredients (except chocolate chips) in a bowl then add wet ingredients. Mix until smooth.

2. Pour batter into a mug and place the chocolate chips in the middle, do not press them down. Drizzle the water on top of the mixture.

3. Microwave for 1 minute 30 seconds or until cake is done and rises to the top of the mug.

4. Let cool before eating.

Chocolate Chip Cookie

Oh, the joy of a sweet, chewy chocolate chip cookie, especially one that's homemade. This chocolate chip cookie in a mug is soft, chewy and only takes 2 minutes!

Cooking time: 1 – 2 minutes

Ingredients:

- 4 tablespoons of all-purpose flour
- 1 egg yolk
- 2 tablespoons of sugar
- 1 tablespoon of milk
- 1 tablespoon of butter, melted
- 1 teaspoon of vanilla
- 2 tablespoons of mini chocolate chips
- A pinch of salt

Instructions:

1. Combine dry ingredients (except chocolate chips) in a bowl then add wet ingredients. Mix until smooth.

2. Pour batter into a mug and fold in chocolate chips.

3. Microwave for 1 minute or until cake is done and cooked through.

S'mores Mug Cake

Ditch the campfire and weekend trips, you can have delicious s'mores made right in a mug in your microwave. A chocolate, marshmallow and graham cracker treat without the pesky bugs.

Cooking time: 2 minutes

Ingredients:

- 3 tablespoons of graham cracker crumbs
- ¼ cup of all-purpose flour
- 1 egg
- 3 tablespoons of sugar
- ¼ teaspoon of baking powder
- 4 tablespoons of butter, melted
- 1 teaspoon of vanilla
- 2 tablespoons of cocoa powder
- ¼ cup of chocolate chips, melted
- 2 tablespoons of marshmallow fluff or 4 large marshmallows
- A pinch of salt

Instructions:

1. Mix graham cracker crumbs with 1 tablespoon of butter and press into bottom of mug.

2. Combine dry ingredients in a bowl then add wet ingredients (except marshmallows). Mix until smooth.

3. Pour half of batter into a mug on top of graham cracker crust and add half of the marshmallow fluff, repeat with remaining batter and marshmallow fluff.

4. Microwave for 1 minute 30 seconds or until cake is done and cooked through.

Brownie Sundae

Another way to satisfy your chocolate craving! A moist fudgy brownie is just perfect.

Cooking time: 2 minutes

Ingredients:

- 5 tablespoons all-purpose flour
- 2 tablespoons of cocoa powder
- 1 tablespoon of milk
- 1 tablespoon of water
- 4 tablespoons of sugar
- 2 tablespoons oil
- A pinch of salt

Instructions:

1. Combine all ingredients in a bowl.

2. Pour into mug.

3. Microwave for 1 – 1 minute 30 seconds, until cooked through.

Conclusion

Well there you have it! You are now officially a mug master, no one can stop you now!

I hope you enjoy my recipes and I hope this book will make your life a little easier. Feel free to spice up recipes and customize them to your liking. You can even challenge yourself to see what you can cook up in a mug on your own.

Author's Afterthoughts

Thanks ever so much to each of my cherished readers for investing the time to read this book!

I know you could have picked from many other books but you chose this one. So a big thanks for downloading this book and reading all the way to the end.

If you enjoyed this book or received value from it, I'd like to ask you for a favor. Please take a few minutes to post an honest and heartfelt review on Amazon.com. Your support does make a difference and helps to benefit other people.

Thanks!

Daniel Humphreys

About the Author

Daniel Humphreys

Many people will ask me if I am German or Norman, and my answer is that I am 100% unique! Joking aside, I owe my cooking influence mainly to my mother who was British! I can certainly make a mean Sheppard's pie, but when it comes to preparing Bratwurst sausages and drinking beer with friends, I am also all in!

I am taking you on this culinary journey with me and hope you can appreciate my diversified background. In my 15 years career as a chef, I never had a dish returned to me by one of clients, so that should say something about me! Actually, I will take that back. My worst critic is my four years old son, who refuses to taste anything that is green color. That shall pass, I am sure.

My hope is to help my children discover the joy of cooking and sharing their creations with their loved ones, like I did all my life. When you develop a passion for cooking and my suspicious is that you have one as well, it usually sticks for life. The best advice I can give anyone as a professional chef is invest. Invest your time, your heart in each meal you are creating. Invest also a little money in good cooking hardware and quality ingredients. But most of all enjoy every meal you prepare with YOUR friends and family!

Made in United States
Orlando, FL
02 December 2021